D0522119

PORTRAIT OF THE BORDERS

This book is dedicated to the life and memories of my mother, Carol Ann Friend (1952-2008), who unfortunately passed away before this project was completed.

'Wherever you are mom, you will always be with me'

PORTRAIT OF THE BORDERS

JASON FRIEND

HALSGROVE

First published in Great Britain in 2008

All images in this book unless otherwise stated are
© Jason Friend/Jason Friend Photography Ltd
All additional images are © David Taylor/www.davidtaylorphotography.co.uk
All images in this book can be licensed via www.jasonfriend.co.uk

All rights reserved. No part of this publication may be reproduced,
stored in a retrieval system, or transmitted in any form or by any
means without the prior permission of the copyright holder.

British Library Cataloguing-in-Publication Data
A CIP record for this title is available from the British Library

ISBN 978 1 84114 721 5

HALSGROVE
Halsgrove House
Ryelands Industrial Estate
Bagley Road, Wellington, Somerset TA21 9PZ
Tel: 01823 653777   Fax: 01823 216796
email: sales@halsgrove.com
website: www.halsgrove.com

Printed and bound by Grafiche Flaminia, Italy

INTRODUCTION

From the rolling hills and rugged coastline of the east to the wild moorlands of the west, the Scottish Borders region is home to an incredible diversity of landscapes.

Found alongside these natural landforms are the remnants of numerous abbeys, castles and hill forts, symbolic of a turbulent history. These natural and historical features have all helped to shape this melting pot of a county. Although perhaps somewhat unfairly overlooked by visitors heading to the highlands, the inhabitants of the region have continued to be fiercely proud of their Scottish heritage and their beloved land.

They have many reasons to be proud of their ancestors, for without them this area may well have become part of England. These lands have seen fierce battles including the two wars of Scottish Independence, as well as other long periods of lawlessness where the inhabitants on both sides of the border were prone to the threats of arson and murder. These troubled times have left their mark on not only the Borders region but also the English language,

with such terms as 'blackmail' being derived from the payments that the working class farmers had to pay to the Border Reivers to protect themselves from pillage and plunder.

For the present day visitor, it is easy to understand why these people fought so hard, often giving their lives to protect their humble homelands. The coastline has to be considered as some of the most impressive to be seen in the British Isles. In particular, the geology to be found near St Abbs is an ever present reminder of the formations that were created when the two separate landmasses that were to become

England and Scotland collided to form the mainland that we know today.

Inland the distinct forms of the Eildon and numerous other hills around the Merse area are the remnants of extinct volcanoes, creating a vista that for any visitor to the area is simply magical. Further west the landscape changes as undulating scenery gives way to more grand hills and numerous lakes are revealed including the mesmerising St Mary's Loch.

The remoteness of the terrain and the constant threat of changeable weather ensures that the Scottish Borders has a distinctly different feel to its English counterpart. As soon as you cross the border from England, influences from the people of the county to the features of the landscape will ensure you undoubtedly experience a Scottish welcome.

Jason Friend

ACKNOWLEDGEMENTS

Completing a project of this size will always require the help and support of numerous people behind the scenes. Personally, the unexpected death of my mother mid-way through the commission meant that I have needed the support and encouragement of my family, friends and business colleagues more than ever.

Thank you to Historic Scotland for allowing me access to photograph the properties under their care, the Scottish Wildlife Trust for their offers of support, David Taylor for the use of a selection of his images, Sam Kellie for enduring the extreme sport of photography, Mark Whitehouse for braving the Scottish winter and lifting my spirits, everybody at the Waverley Bar in Hawick for their encouragement and Steven Pugsley and the rest of the team at Halsgrove for making this book a reality.

Personally this book would have never been without the love and support of my fiancée, Lynette Whitehouse, and my father John Friend. A huge thank you to all of my friends who were there when I needed them the most including Jason Haynes, Wayne Hackeson, Steven Turner and Steve Hawthorne. A special thank you to the Whitehouse family for always believing in me.

MAP

Sunrise reflected in the tranquil waters of the Alemoor Loch, a popular place for recreational fishing near the town of Hawick.

A statue of William Wallace located near Scott's View and Dryburgh.

The Eildon Hills and the River Tweed, viewed in autumn from
the famous viewpoint of Scott's View near Newton St Boswells.

A rocky stretch of the Ettrick Water,
surrounded by a pocket of woodland.

Breaking light illuminates a tree and reeds on the banks of the River Tweed, against a backdrop of an indigo sky.

Celtic design on a war memorial cross within
the grounds of the church of Ladykirk.

Jedburgh Abbey and surrounding gardens.

Sunset above Kyles Hill, in the area known as the
Merse.

Wind farms are a controversial new feature to be found increasingly within the Scottish landscape. This wind turbine is part of the Dun Law wind farm located at the western end of the Lammermuir Hills.

Poplar trees growing in the Mertoun Estate
near the town of St Boswells.

Mist begins to shroud the rolling hills of the Scottish Uplands, viewed from the low level route of the Pennine Way near Kirk Yetholm.

The town of Peebles, with the Glentress Forest in the distance.

A shaft of light gently
illuminates fields to be found
near the town of Peebles.

Detail of a pine cone on a bed of moss.

A forest path running through the Cardrona Forest,
a mixed conifer woodland popular with hikers.

The gentle curve of Ettrick Water through
farmland in the Ettrick Valley.

Bronze statue celebrating the historical hero of the coastal town of Eyemouth, Willie Spears (1812 - 1885). Willie became famous when he revolted against the Church of Scotland for the high taxes placed on the town's fishermen and their catch.

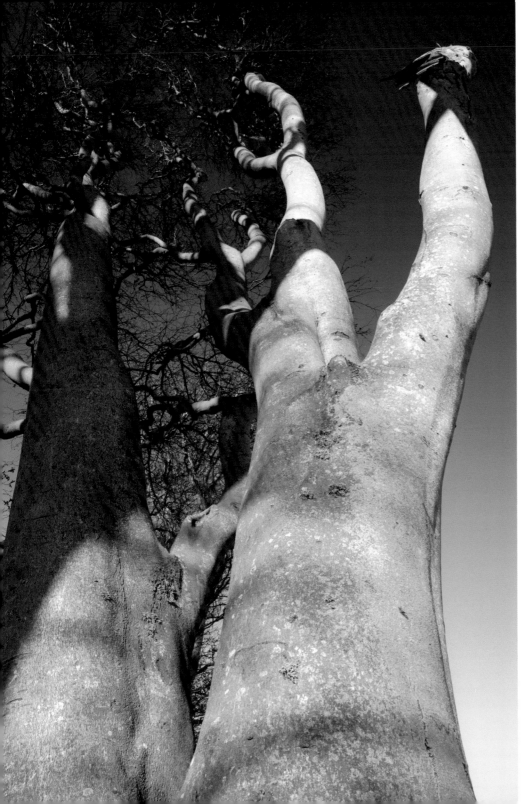

A weathered tree stands proud near the town of Duns.

Opposite page: The new parish church in the village of Ayton.

Field of oil seed rape blowing in a
breeze, looking towards Teviot Dale.
(Photo: David Taylor)

Patterns in agricultural land near Hareheugh.

The gentle flowing rapids of
Leithen Water.

Opposite page: Hazy sunset looking
towards the Eildon Hills from
near the town of Duns.

Tima Water meanders through Craik Forest.

Moss-covered tree branch, stretching across a small burn.

Ladder stile over a wall marking the England/
Scotland border, with the Schil in the distance.

Looking towards the rolling hills
of the Scottish Borders from the
viewpoint at the Carter Bar
border crossing as heading
north from England.

Dramatic skies over Lindean Loch,
Whitlaw Mosses National Nature Reserve.

Tree and lake in the Monteviot Estate
near the Harestanes Visitors Centre.

(Photo: David Taylor)

A stone bridge over the fast-flowing waters of the River Ettrick.

Hermitage Water running in front of the Hermitage Castle. The castle has a somewhat colourful history with numerous stories of war, treason and murder being associated with the property. It was built in an area considered to be a key element in the English and Scottish wars for control over the Liddesdale and the border area.

Example of a traditional dry stone wall in Wauchope Forest.

Close up view of a wooden sculpture in the Thornielee Forest, part of the Tweed Valley Forest Park located in the main woodland corridor between Peebles and Selkirk.

'Lilliard's Stone', a grave marker from 1544 commemorating the death of Maid Lilliard who died during the Battle of Ancrum.

(Photo: David Taylor)

A small group of trees located on a hill above the town of Duns, looking towards England and the Cheviot Hills.

Panoramic view of the Tweed Valley, viewed from near Walkerburn.

Autumn mists clear
from woodland above
the River Tweed.

Single track road heading towards
the St Abbs lighthouse, through the
St Abbs National Nature Reserve.

Opposite page: Sunrise over the North
Sea near the village of Burnmouth –
the first settlement to be found in
Scotland after crossing the English
border near the coast.

The River Tweed near the small village of
Walkerburn in the Tweed Valley.

Detail of a fast flowing stream found in Liddesdale.

Inscription on a memorial stone celebrating
the formation of the Coldstream Guards.

The town houses and monuments of Coldstream,
located on the banks of the River Tweed.

The wooden path between Maxton and the River Tweed, for people walking the Saint Cuthbert's Way long distance trail.
(Photo: David Taylor)

The felling of trees is a common sight in the Borders region. The wild, open terrain of the region provides a number of suitable locations for forest plantations. Although these were originally conceived as a means to guarantee a steady supply of timber in the event of another war, they now also provide numerous opportunities for outdoor recreation and conservation projects such as the preservation of the native Red Squirrel.

Undulating hills and cliffs along the east coast, looking north from the St Abbs National Nature Reserve.

Waves crashing against
rocky outcrops near the
harbour of St Abbs.

Rolling hills and forest plantation near
the Dumfries and Galloway border in
the Liddesdale area.

A small pocket of woodland
near to Duns Castle.

A blizzard engulfs a farm house situated near
the remote Glenlude Hill.

A fresh snowfall transforms
the humble Whitrope Burn.

A typical example of a stone-arched bridge to be found in the Borders region, spanning the Whiteadder Water near Duns.

Newcastleton is a fine example of an
eighteenth-century planned village, located in
the picturesque Liddesdale. Designed to a plan
by William Keir of Whithaugh for the third
Duke of Buccleuch, the streets and squares of
the town are all based around a grid system
offering ample open spaces.

The ruins of Cessford Castle,
near the town of Morebattle.

(Photo: David Taylor)

Shadow of a lamp on the
walls of Coldingham Priory.

The River Tweed dominates the landscape near Coldstream, the self-proclaimed first true border 'toon'.

View from window in Greenknowe Tower,
framed by the stone of the building.

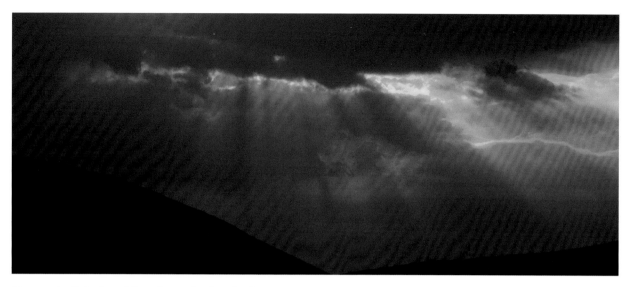

Dramatic light breaking through clouds above the Scottish Uplands, viewed from the low level route of the Pennine Way near Kirk Yetholm.

Panoramic view of the Harelaw Moor region.

Passing light on the slopes of Fethan Hill.

Mirror reflection of woodland in the still waters of the Alemoor Loch.

Winter storms create a huge swell
in the North Sea near St Abbs.

The St Abbs lighthouse, erected in
1862 after the sinking of the *Martello*
on Carr Rock five years previously.

Lone tree in a field of barley between
Brownrigg and Cessford Moor.

(Photo: David Taylor)

Early morning light softly illuminates a group of trees on the edge of the Craik Forest.

The magnificent ruins of Melrose Abbey,
considered to be the final resting place of the
heart of Robert the Bruce.

Sir Walter Scott monument and
Town Hall clock situated in the
market place of Selkirk.

Looking across the River Tweed, the natural border between England and Scotland.

Riverside path running by the River Tweed,
in the town of Peebles.

The famous Grey Mares Tail waterfall, located near the Dumfries and Galloway/ Scottish Borders county border.

Sunset on the banks of the River Blackadder
in the south east Borders region.

The impressive Mertoun Bridge spanning the
River Tweed near St Boswells.

Greenknowe Tower, a typical
example of a tower-house. The
tower-house was the traditional
home of the Scottish Laird.

A field of barley on the Monteviot Estate near Ancrum. (Photo: David Taylor)

A lone tree and hills near the town of Peebles.

Sunset over the hills of Liddesdale
near the English border.

Breaking light illuminates the autumn colours of
the tree-clad hills surrounding St Mary's Loch.

Looking towards the town of Kelso
from the Millennium Viewpoint.

The Crystal Well, a clear
spring that runs into the
River Tweed near Maxton.

(Photo: David Taylor)

Gale force winds create large swells in the
North Sea, demonstrating the importance of
the sea wall defences in place at Eyemouth Bay.

Uplifted rock layers at Petticot Wick near St Abbs.

The Waterloo monument at
the summit of Peniel Heugh.
(Photo: David Taylor)

Nature begins to reclaim a
disused stone farm building
in the Ettrick Valley.

Sheep grazing on pasture land in the Ettrick Valley.

Deciduous trees found at Cragbank Woods National Nature Reserve. This protected woodland is the largest area of ancient ash, elm and hazel woodland left in the Scottish Borders.

Stained glass window in Bowden Kirk. The window, known as the Priest's Door Window, commemorates military deaths in the early twentieth century.

(Photo: David Taylor)

The dramatic ruins of Kelso Abbey. Sir Walter Scott
described the architecture as the most beautiful in Scotland.

Weathered paint work on the hull of a fishing
boat moored in the harbour of St Abbs.

Dawn light bathes the rocky shoreline and coastal homes of the inhabitants of Burnmouth.

Farmhouse and fields, looking west from
the St Abbs National Nature Reserve.

Hay bales stacked outside
a barn near Duns.

Farm gate and undulating scenery near Liddesdale.

Autumnal beech trees in Blindwells
Plantation near Crailing.

(Photo: David Taylor)

Lone trees cling for survival on the rocky crags of Hareheugh.

A breaking storm reveals a dusting of snow on the Moorfoot Hills. The popular Glentress Forest can be seen in the foreground.

Mounted Border Reiver monument outside the Burgh Chambers in Galashiels.

Opposite page: The grand architecture of Jedburgh Abbey.

Sea fishing lobster pots stacked in the harbour of Eyemouth.

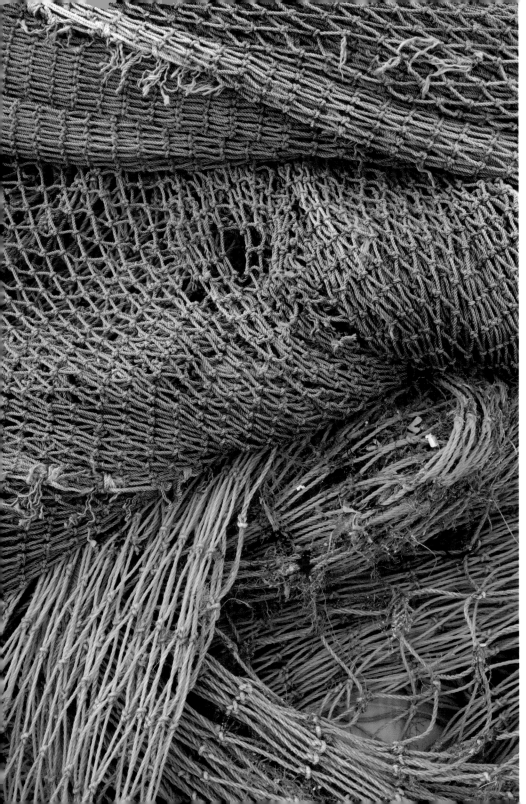

Entwined fishing nets stored in the harbour of Eyemouth.

Sun breaking though a storm highlights the features
of the uplands to be found near Blake Muir.

The rocky crags of Hareheugh.

Snow on high land near Carter Bar on the English border, looking towards the rolling hills of Scotland.

Opposite page: A thick coat of wool helps to ensure that grazing sheep can survive the hostile environment of the winter months in the Scottish Borders.

A sprinkle of snow on the slopes of Leithen Hopes.

Sunrise reflected in Mire Loch, near the
dramatic coastline of St Abbs Head.

The B 7009 heading towards Selkirk meanders
through picturesque Borders' scenery.

The shape of a lone tree sculpted by the wind, with agricultural land and the famous Eildon Hills in the distance.

Smeaton's seven-arched bridge near Coldstream, was constructed between 1763 to 1766. Robert Burns famously crossed the bridge into England for the first time on 7 May 1787. A plaque on the bridge commemorates this alongside a prayer for blessing that he made on the day before entering the foreign land –

'O Scotia ! My dear, my native soil!
For whom my warmest wish to heaven is sent!
Long may thy hardy sons of rustic toil be blest
with health, and peace, and sweet content.'

Details of a grand
wooden door at
Coldingham Priory.

Style over a dry stone wall leading to the summit of
Wideopen Hill, on the St Cuthbert's long distance trail.
(Photo: David Taylor)

The well-preserved remains of Smailholm Tower. The location of the rectangular tower on a hilly outcrop ensures that it dominates the surrounding landscape for miles.

Gentle morning light bathes a small pocket of woodland.

Liddel Water flowing through
a bridge in Liddesdale.

Morning light scattered across tussock land and a lone tree, beneath the shadow of border upland.

Opposite page: Sunset behind the Scottish Upland Hills near Kirk Yetholm, on the final stretch of the Pennine Way.

Typical Borders' scene of farmland,
plantation and rolling upland hills.

Coldingham Priory, in the historic town of Coldingham.

Storm clouds clear from above the sandy
beach to be found at Coldingham Bay.

The rocky coastline of the St Abbs National Nature Reserve.

Close up view of moss. The clean air and damp environment of the Scottish Borders provides a perfect growing environment for such plants.

Moss-covered tree in Wauchope Forest.

Forest plantation sandwiched between moors
and land used for agricultural purposes.

Fast-flowing stream shortly before it joins Borthwick Water near Roberton.

131

Wind-damaged tree covered in moss on the floor of a plantation in Wauchope Forest.

Opposite page: An inquisitive Robin rests on a branch in woodland near Alemoor Loch.

133

Shafts of light break through storm clouds near Harelaw Moor.

Grand house located in forest plantation east of Gala Water.

A public footbridge crossing the
Kirk Burn in the Forest of Cardrona.

The parish church of Earlston, a small
village located north of Melrose.

Farmland in the hills in the vicinity of Peebles.

Trees on the banks of the Hermitage Water.

Looking across the skyline of the historic town of Hawick. Possibly the most charismatic of the border towns with the popular Hawick Common Riding Festival having been described as one of the greatest parties to be found in the world. The event which is held in the June of each year celebrates the capturing of the English flag from a group of raiders by local Hawick youths back in 1514.

Snow-engulfed forest plantation near the
Carter Bar England/Scotland border.

St Mary's Loch at dusk.

Cotton grass on moorland near the English border.

A rainbow above the Schil on the England/Scotland border.